The Standard®

EASA FCL-COMPLIANT PILOT LOG

ASA-SP-EASA

THE STANDARD® EASA FCL-COMPLIANT PILOT LOG
SP-EASA

ASA-SP-EASA
ISBN 978-1-61945-623-3

Printed in Korea

[18] 24

Aviation Supplies & Academics, Inc.
7005 132nd Place SE
Newcastle, Washington 98059 USA
asa2fly.com | asa@asa2fly.com

TRANSPORTATION

ISBN 978-1-61954-623-3

51995 >

9 781619 546233

The Standard EASA FCL-Compliant Pilot Log

Name ______________________ **Licence Number** ______________ **Logbook Number** ______________

Mailing Address ______________________________________ **From** ______________

____ **To** ______________

Licences Held

Type	Date Issued	Licence Number
STUDENT PILOT		
LAPL		
PPL		
CPL		
ATPL		
MPL		
FLIGHT INSTRUCTOR		
GROUND INSTRUCTOR		
AIRCRAFT MECHANIC		

Rating Record

☐ AIRPLANE ☐ BALLOON

☐ HELICOPTER ☐ SAILPLANE

☐ POWERED PARACHUTE ☐ WEIGHT-SHIFT CONTROL

☐ INSTRUMENT

☐ NIGHT

☐ AEROBATICS

☐ MOUNTAIN

☐ FI ☐ IRA

☐ ______________

☐ ______________

☐ ______________

☐ ______________

☐ ______________

☐ ______________

Aircraft Type Ratings

____

____

____

____

____

____

____

____

____

____

____

____

____

____

Instructions For Use

FCL.050 Recording of flight time

The pilot shall keep a reliable record of the details of all flights flown in a form and manner established by the competent authority.

(a) The record of the flights flown should contain at least the following information:

- (1) personal details: name(s) and address of the pilot;
- (2) for each flight:
  - (i) name(s) of PIC;
  - (ii) date of flight;
  - (iii) place and time of departure and arrival;
  - (iv) type, including make, model and variant, and registration of the aircraft;
  - (v) indication if the aircraft is SE or ME, if applicable;
  - (vi) total time of flight;
  - (vii) accumulated total time of flight.
- (3) for each FSTD session, if applicable:
  - (i) type and qualification number of the training device;
  - (ii) FSTD instruction;
  - (iii) date;
  - (iv) total time of session;
  - (v) accumulated total time.
- (4) details on pilot function, namely PIC, including solo, SPIC and PICUS time, co-pilot, dual, FI or FE;
- (5) Operational conditions, namely if the operation takes place at night, or is conducted under instrument flight rules.

(b) Logging of time:

- (1) PIC flight time:
  - (i) the holder of a licence may log as PIC time all of the flight time during which he or she is the PIC;
  - (ii) the applicant for, or holder of, a pilot licence may log as PIC time all solo flight time, flight time as SPIC and flight time under supervision provided that such SPIC time and flight time under supervision are countersigned by the instructor;
  - (iii) the holder of an instructor certificate may log as PIC all flight time during which he or she acts as an instructor in an aircraft;
  - (iv) the holder of an examiner's certificate may log as PIC all flight time during which he or she occupies a pilot's seat and acts as an examiner in an aircraft;
  - (v) a co-pilot acting as PICUS on an aircraft on which more than one pilot is required under the type certification of the aircraft or as required by operational requirements provided that such PICUS time is countersigned by the PIC;
  - (vi) if the holder of a pilot licence carries out a number of flights upon the same day returning on each occasion to the same place of departure and the interval between successive flights does not exceed 30 minutes, such series of flights may be recorded as a single entry;
  - (vii) where Regulation (EU) No 965/2012 requires the pilot to act as PIC under the supervision of another pilot (supervisor), both the pilot and the supervisor may log the flight time as PIC.
- (2) co-pilot flight time: the holder of a pilot licence occupying a pilot seat as co-pilot may log all flight time as co-pilot flight time on an aircraft on which more than one pilot is required under the type certification of the aircraft, the regulations or the operations manual of the operator under which the flight is conducted;
- (3) cruise relief co-pilot flight time: a cruise relief co-pilot may log all flight time as co-pilot when occupying a pilot's seat;
- (4) instruction time: a summary of all time logged by an applicant for a licence or rating as flight instruction, instrument flight instruction, instrument ground time, etc., may be logged if certified by the appropriately rated or authorised instructor from whom it was received;
- (5) PICUS flight time: provided that the method of supervision is acceptable to the competent authority, a co-pilot may log as PIC flight time flown as PICUS when all the duties and functions of PIC on that flight were carried out in such a way that the intervention of the PIC in the interest of safety was not required.

(c) Format of the record:

- (1) details of flights flown under commercial air transport may be recorded in an electronic format maintained by the operator.
  In this case an operator should make the records of all flights operated by the pilot, including differences and familiarisation training, available upon request to the flight crew member concerned;
- (2) for other types of flights in aeroplanes, helicopters and powered-lift aircraft, the pilot should record the details of the flights flown in the following logbook format, which may be kept in electronic format. All data set out in (a) should be included.
- (3) For sailplanes, balloons and airships, a suitable format, which may be electric, should be used. That format should contain the relevant items mentioned in (a) and additional information specific to the type of operation.

(d) FCL.050 requires holders of a pilot licence to record details of all flights flown. This logbook enables pilot licence holders to record flying experience in a manner which will facilitate this process while providing a permanent record of the licence holders flying. Pilots who fly regularly aeroplanes and helicopters or other aircraft categories are recommended to maintain separate logbooks for each aircraft category.

(e) Flight crew logbook entries should be made as soon as practicable after any flight undertaken. All entries in the flight crew logbook should comply with the following:

(1) in case of paper records, they should be made in ink or indelible pencil; or

(2) in case of electronic records, they should be made and kept in a way to be readily available at the request of a competent authority, and contain all relevant items that are mentioned in (a), certified by the pilot, and in a format acceptable by the competent authority.

(f) The particulars of every flight in the course of which the holder of a flight crew licence acts as a member of the operating crew of an aircraft are to be recorded in the appropriate columns using one line for each flight, provided that if an aircraft carries out a number of flights upon the same day returning on each occasion to the same place of departure and the interval between successive flights does not exceed 30 minutes, such series of flights may be recorded as a single entry.

(g) Flight time is recorded:

(1) for aeroplanes, touring motor gliders and powered-lift aircraft, from the moment an aircraft first moves to taking off until the moment it finally comes to rest at the end of the flight;

(2) for helicopters, from the moment a helicopter's rotor blades start turning until the moment the helicopter finally comes to rest at the end of the flight, and the rotor blades are stopped;

(3) for airships, from the moment an airship is released from the mast to taking off until the moment the airship finally comes to rest at the end of the flight, and is secured on the mast;

(h) When an aircraft carries two or more pilots as members of the operating crew, one of them shall, before the flight commences, be designated by the operator as the aircraft PIC, according to operational requirements, who may delegate the conduct of the flight to another suitably qualified pilot. All flying carried out as PIC is entered in the logbook as 'PIC'. A pilot flying as 'PICUS' or 'SPIC' enters flying time as 'PIC' but all such entries are to be certified by the PIC or FI in the 'Remarks' column of the logbook.

[FCL.050 regulation revised for use with this ASA EASA logbook.]

(i) Notes on recording of flight time:

column 1: enter the date (dd/mm/yy) on which the flight commences;

column 2 and 3: enter the place of departure and destination either in full or the internationally recognised three or four letter designator. All times should be in UTC;

column 4: enter the aircraft make, model, variant, including the registration number.

column 5: enter the name(s) of PIC or SELF as appropriate;

column 6 and 7: indicate whether the operation was SP or MP, and for SP operation whether SE or ME;

column 8: total time of flight may be entered in hours and minutes or decimal notation as desired;

column 9: indicate the number of landings as pilot flying by day or night;

column 10: enter flight time condition undertaken at night or under instrument flight rules if applicable;

column 11: pilot function time:

(i) enter flight time as PIC, SPIC and PICUS as PIC;

(ii) all time recorded as SPIC or PICUS is countersigned by the aircraft PIC/FI in the 'remarks' (column 12);

(iii) instructor time should be recorded as appropriate and also entered as PIC.

column 12: FSTD:

(i) for any FSTD enter the type of aircraft and qualification number of the device. For other flight training devices enter either FNPT I or FNPT II as appropriate;

(ii) total time of session includes all exercises carried out in the device, including pre- and after-flight checks;

(iii) enter the type of exercise performed in the 'remarks' (column 12), for example operator proficiency check, revalidation.

column 13: the 'remarks and endorsements' column may be used to record details of the flight at the holder's discretion. The following entries, however, should always be made:

(i) instrument flight time undertaken as part of the training for a licence or rating;

(ii) details of all skill tests and proficiency checks;

(iii) name and signature of PIC if the pilot is recording flight time as SPIC or PICUS;

(iv) name and signature of instructor if flight is part of an SEP or TMG class rating revalidation;

(v) for multi-pilot operations in single-pilot helicopters, the form of operation, name and signature of the examiner conducting the skill test or proficiency check or operator proficiency check, and the name of the operator in the case of the operator proficiency check.

(j) When each page is completed, accumulated flight time or hours should be entered in the appropriate columns and certified by the pilot in the 'remarks and endorsements' column.

DATE (DD/MM/YY)	DEPARTURE		ARRIVAL		AIRCRAFT		NAME(S) PIC	SINGLE PILOT TIME		MULTI PILOT TIME		TOTAL TIME OF FLIGHT		NO. LDG.	
	PLACE	TIME (hh:mm)	PLACE	TIME (hh:mm)	MAKE, MODEL, VARIANT	REGISTRATION		SE	ME					DAY	NIGHT
							TOTAL FROM THIS PAGE								
							TOTAL FROM PREVIOUS PAGE								
							TOTAL TO DATE								

CONDITIONS OF FLIGHT				PILOT FUNCTION TIME				FSTD SESSION			REMARKS AND ENDORSEMENTS
NIGHT	IFR		FLIGHT RULES	PIC	CO-PILOT	DUAL	FI	DATE (DD/MM/YY)	TYPE	TOTAL TIME OF SESSION	
	HOOD	ACTUAL									

I certify that the statements made by me on this form are true.

PILOT'S SIGNATURE

DATE (DD/MM/YY)	DEPARTURE		ARRIVAL		AIRCRAFT		NAME(S) PIC	SINGLE PILOT TIME		MULTI PILOT TIME		TOTAL TIME OF FLIGHT		NO. LDG.	
	PLACE	TIME (hh:mm)	PLACE	TIME (hh:mm)	MAKE, MODEL, VARIANT	REGISTRATION		SE	ME					DAY	NIGHT
							TOTAL FROM THIS PAGE								
							TOTAL FROM PREVIOUS PAGE								
							TOTAL TO DATE								

CONDITIONS OF FLIGHT				PILOT FUNCTION TIME				FSTD SESSION			REMARKS AND ENDORSEMENTS
NIGHT	IFR		FLIGHT RULES	PIC	CO-PILOT	DUAL	FI	DATE (DD/MM/YY)	TYPE	TOTAL TIME OF SESSION	
	HOOD	ACTUAL									

I certify that the statements made by me on this form are true.

PILOT'S SIGNATURE

DATE (DD/MM/YY)	DEPARTURE		ARRIVAL		AIRCRAFT		NAME(S) PIC	SINGLE PILOT TIME		MULTI PILOT TIME	TOTAL TIME OF FLIGHT	NO. LDG.	
	PLACE	TIME (hh:mm)	PLACE	TIME (hh:mm)	MAKE, MODEL, VARIANT	REGISTRATION		SE	ME			DAY	NIGHT
							TOTAL FROM THIS PAGE						
							TOTAL FROM PREVIOUS PAGE						
							TOTAL TO DATE						

CONDITIONS OF FLIGHT							PILOT FUNCTION TIME								FSTD SESSION				REMARKS AND ENDORSEMENTS
NIGHT		IFR				FLIGHT RULES	PIC		CO-PILOT		DUAL		FI		DATE (DD/MM/YY)	TYPE	TOTAL TIME OF SESSION		
		HOOD		ACTUAL															

I certify that the statements made by me on this form are true.

PILOT'S SIGNATURE

DATE (DD/MM/YY)	DEPARTURE		ARRIVAL		AIRCRAFT		NAME(S) PIC	SINGLE PILOT TIME		MULTI PILOT TIME		TOTAL TIME OF FLIGHT		NO. LDG.	
	PLACE	TIME (hh:mm)	PLACE	TIME (hh:mm)	MAKE, MODEL, VARIANT	REGISTRATION		SE	ME					DAY	NIGHT
							TOTAL FROM THIS PAGE								
							TOTAL FROM PREVIOUS PAGE								
							TOTAL TO DATE								

CONDITIONS OF FLIGHT							PILOT FUNCTION TIME								FSTD SESSION				REMARKS AND ENDORSEMENTS
NIGHT		IFR				FLIGHT RULES	PIC		CO-PILOT		DUAL		FI		DATE (DD/MM/YY)	TYPE	TOTAL TIME OF SESSION		
		HOOD		ACTUAL															
																			I certify that the statements made by me on this form are true.
																			PILOT'S SIGNATURE

DATE (DD/MM/YY)	DEPARTURE		ARRIVAL		AIRCRAFT		NAME(S) PIC	SINGLE PILOT TIME		MULTI PILOT TIME		TOTAL TIME OF FLIGHT		NO. LDG.	
	PLACE	TIME (hh:mm)	PLACE	TIME (hh:mm)	MAKE, MODEL, VARIANT	REGISTRATION		SE	ME					DAY	NIGHT
							TOTAL FROM THIS PAGE								
							TOTAL FROM PREVIOUS PAGE								
							TOTAL TO DATE								

CONDITIONS OF FLIGHT				PILOT FUNCTION TIME				FSTD SESSION			REMARKS AND ENDORSEMENTS
NIGHT	IFR		FLIGHT RULES	PIC	CO-PILOT	DUAL	FI	DATE (DD/MM/YY)	TYPE	TOTAL TIME OF SESSION	
	HOOD	ACTUAL									
											I certify that the statements made by me on this form are true.
											PILOT'S SIGNATURE

DATE (DD/MM/YY)	DEPARTURE		ARRIVAL		AIRCRAFT		NAME(S) PIC	SINGLE PILOT TIME		MULTI PILOT TIME		TOTAL TIME OF FLIGHT		NO. LDG.	
	PLACE	TIME (hh:mm)	PLACE	TIME (hh:mm)	MAKE, MODEL, VARIANT	REGISTRATION		SE	ME					DAY	NIGHT
							TOTAL FROM THIS PAGE								
							TOTAL FROM PREVIOUS PAGE								
							TOTAL TO DATE								

CONDITIONS OF FLIGHT							PILOT FUNCTION TIME								FSTD SESSION				REMARKS AND ENDORSEMENTS
NIGHT		IFR				FLIGHT RULES	PIC		CO-PILOT		DUAL		FI		DATE (DD/MM/YY)	TYPE	TOTAL TIME OF SESSION		
		HOOD		ACTUAL															
																			I certify that the statements made by me on this form are true.
																			PILOT'S SIGNATURE

DATE (DD/MM/YY)	DEPARTURE		ARRIVAL		AIRCRAFT		NAME(S) PIC	SINGLE PILOT TIME		MULTI PILOT TIME		TOTAL TIME OF FLIGHT		NO. LDG.	
	PLACE	TIME (hh:mm)	PLACE	TIME (hh:mm)	MAKE, MODEL, VARIANT	REGISTRATION		SE	ME					DAY	NIGHT
							TOTAL FROM THIS PAGE								
							TOTAL FROM PREVIOUS PAGE								
							TOTAL TO DATE								

CONDITIONS OF FLIGHT							PILOT FUNCTION TIME								FSTD SESSION				REMARKS AND ENDORSEMENTS
NIGHT		IFR				FLIGHT RULES	PIC		CO-PILOT		DUAL		FI		DATE (DD/MM/YY)	TYPE	TOTAL TIME OF SESSION		
		HOOD		ACTUAL															
																			I certify that the statements made by me on this form are true.
																			PILOT'S SIGNATURE

DATE (DD/MM/YY)	DEPARTURE		ARRIVAL		AIRCRAFT		NAME(S) PIC	SINGLE PILOT TIME		MULTI PILOT TIME		TOTAL TIME OF FLIGHT		NO. LDG.	
	PLACE	TIME (hh:mm)	PLACE	TIME (hh:mm)	MAKE, MODEL, VARIANT	REGISTRATION		SE	ME					DAY	NIGHT
							TOTAL FROM THIS PAGE								
							TOTAL FROM PREVIOUS PAGE								
							TOTAL TO DATE								

CONDITIONS OF FLIGHT							PILOT FUNCTION TIME								FSTD SESSION				REMARKS AND ENDORSEMENTS
NIGHT		IFR				FLIGHT RULES	PIC		CO-PILOT		DUAL		FI		DATE (DD/MM/YY)	TYPE	TOTAL TIME OF SESSION		
		HOOD		ACTUAL															

I certify that the statements made by me on this form are true.

PILOT'S SIGNATURE

DATE (DD/MM/YY)	DEPARTURE		ARRIVAL		AIRCRAFT		NAME(S) PIC	SINGLE PILOT TIME		MULTI PILOT TIME		TOTAL TIME OF FLIGHT		NO. LDG.	
	PLACE	TIME (hh:mm)	PLACE	TIME (hh:mm)	MAKE, MODEL, VARIANT	REGISTRATION		SE	ME					DAY	NIGHT
							TOTAL FROM THIS PAGE								
							TOTAL FROM PREVIOUS PAGE								
							TOTAL TO DATE								

CONDITIONS OF FLIGHT							PILOT FUNCTION TIME								FSTD SESSION				REMARKS AND ENDORSEMENTS
NIGHT		IFR				FLIGHT RULES	PIC		CO-PILOT		DUAL		FI		DATE (DD/MM/YY)	TYPE	TOTAL TIME OF SESSION		
		HOOD		ACTUAL															
																			I certify that the statements made by me on this form are true.
																			PILOT'S SIGNATURE

DATE (DD/MM/YY)	DEPARTURE		ARRIVAL		AIRCRAFT		NAME(S) PIC	SINGLE PILOT TIME		MULTI PILOT TIME		TOTAL TIME OF FLIGHT		NO. LDG.	
	PLACE	TIME (hh:mm)	PLACE	TIME (hh:mm)	MAKE, MODEL, VARIANT	REGISTRATION		SE	ME					DAY	NIGHT
							TOTAL FROM THIS PAGE								
							TOTAL FROM PREVIOUS PAGE								
							TOTAL TO DATE								

CONDITIONS OF FLIGHT				PILOT FUNCTION TIME				FSTD SESSION			REMARKS AND ENDORSEMENTS
NIGHT	IFR		FLIGHT RULES	PIC	CO-PILOT	DUAL	FI	DATE (DD/MM/YY)	TYPE	TOTAL TIME OF SESSION	
	HOOD	ACTUAL									
											I certify that the statements made by me on this form are true.
											PILOT'S SIGNATURE

DATE (DD/MM/YY)	DEPARTURE		ARRIVAL		AIRCRAFT		NAME(S) PIC	SINGLE PILOT TIME		MULTI PILOT TIME		TOTAL TIME OF FLIGHT		NO. LDG.	
	PLACE	TIME (hh:mm)	PLACE	TIME (hh:mm)	MAKE, MODEL, VARIANT	REGISTRATION		SE	ME					DAY	NIGHT
							TOTAL FROM THIS PAGE								
							TOTAL FROM PREVIOUS PAGE								
							TOTAL TO DATE								

CONDITIONS OF FLIGHT							PILOT FUNCTION TIME								FSTD SESSION				REMARKS AND ENDORSEMENTS
NIGHT		IFR				FLIGHT RULES	PIC		CO-PILOT		DUAL		FI		DATE (DD/MM/YY)	TYPE	TOTAL TIME OF SESSION		
		HOOD		ACTUAL															
																			I certify that the statements made by me on this form are true.
																			PILOT'S SIGNATURE

DATE (DD/MM/YY)	DEPARTURE		ARRIVAL		AIRCRAFT		NAME(S) PIC	SINGLE PILOT TIME		MULTI PILOT TIME		TOTAL TIME OF FLIGHT		NO. LDG.	
	PLACE	TIME (hh:mm)	PLACE	TIME (hh:mm)	MAKE, MODEL, VARIANT	REGISTRATION		SE	ME					DAY	NIGHT
							TOTAL FROM THIS PAGE								
							TOTAL FROM PREVIOUS PAGE								
							TOTAL TO DATE								

CONDITIONS OF FLIGHT				PILOT FUNCTION TIME				FSTD SESSION			REMARKS AND ENDORSEMENTS
NIGHT	IFR		FLIGHT RULES	PIC	CO-PILOT	DUAL	FI	DATE (DD/MM/YY)	TYPE	TOTAL TIME OF SESSION	
	HOOD	ACTUAL									
											I certify that the statements made by me on this form are true.
											PILOT'S SIGNATURE

DATE (DD/MM/YY)	DEPARTURE		ARRIVAL		AIRCRAFT		NAME(S) PIC	SINGLE PILOT TIME		MULTI PILOT TIME		TOTAL TIME OF FLIGHT		NO. LDG.	
	PLACE	TIME (hh:mm)	PLACE	TIME (hh:mm)	MAKE, MODEL, VARIANT	REGISTRATION		SE	ME					DAY	NIGHT
							TOTAL FROM THIS PAGE								
							TOTAL FROM PREVIOUS PAGE								
							TOTAL TO DATE								

CONDITIONS OF FLIGHT				PILOT FUNCTION TIME				FSTD SESSION			REMARKS AND ENDORSEMENTS
NIGHT	IFR		FLIGHT RULES	PIC	CO-PILOT	DUAL	FI	DATE (DD/MM/YY)	TYPE	TOTAL TIME OF SESSION	
	HOOD	ACTUAL									
											I certify that the statements made by me on this form are true.
											PILOT'S SIGNATURE

DATE (DD/MM/YY)	DEPARTURE		ARRIVAL		AIRCRAFT		NAME(S) PIC	SINGLE PILOT TIME		MULTI PILOT TIME		TOTAL TIME OF FLIGHT		NO. LDG.	
	PLACE	TIME (hh:mm)	PLACE	TIME (hh:mm)	MAKE, MODEL, VARIANT	REGISTRATION		SE	ME					DAY	NIGHT
							TOTAL FROM THIS PAGE								
							TOTAL FROM PREVIOUS PAGE								
							TOTAL TO DATE								

CONDITIONS OF FLIGHT				PILOT FUNCTION TIME				FSTD SESSION			REMARKS AND ENDORSEMENTS
NIGHT	IFR		FLIGHT RULES	PIC	CO-PILOT	DUAL	FI	DATE (DD/MM/YY)	TYPE	TOTAL TIME OF SESSION	
	HOOD	ACTUAL									

I certify that the statements made by me on this form are true.

PILOT'S SIGNATURE

DATE (DD/MM/YY)	DEPARTURE		ARRIVAL		AIRCRAFT		NAME(S) PIC	SINGLE PILOT TIME		MULTI PILOT TIME		TOTAL TIME OF FLIGHT		NO. LDG.	
	PLACE	TIME (hh:mm)	PLACE	TIME (hh:mm)	MAKE, MODEL, VARIANT	REGISTRATION		SE	ME					DAY	NIGHT
							TOTAL FROM THIS PAGE								
							TOTAL FROM PREVIOUS PAGE								
							TOTAL TO DATE								

CONDITIONS OF FLIGHT							PILOT FUNCTION TIME								FSTD SESSION				REMARKS AND ENDORSEMENTS
NIGHT		IFR				FLIGHT RULES	PIC		CO-PILOT		DUAL		FI		DATE (DD/MM/YY)	TYPE	TOTAL TIME OF SESSION		
		HOOD		ACTUAL															
																			I certify that the statements made by me on this form are true.
																			PILOT'S SIGNATURE

DATE (DD/MM/YY)	DEPARTURE		ARRIVAL		AIRCRAFT		NAME(S) PIC	SINGLE PILOT TIME		MULTI PILOT TIME		TOTAL TIME OF FLIGHT		NO. LDG.	
	PLACE	TIME (hh:mm)	PLACE	TIME (hh:mm)	MAKE, MODEL, VARIANT	REGISTRATION		SE	ME					DAY	NIGHT
							TOTAL FROM THIS PAGE								
							TOTAL FROM PREVIOUS PAGE								
							TOTAL TO DATE								

CONDITIONS OF FLIGHT							PILOT FUNCTION TIME								FSTD SESSION				REMARKS AND ENDORSEMENTS
NIGHT		IFR				FLIGHT RULES	PIC		CO-PILOT		DUAL		FI		DATE (DD/MM/YY)	TYPE	TOTAL TIME OF SESSION		
		HOOD		ACTUAL															
																			I certify that the statements made by me on this form are true.
																			PILOT'S SIGNATURE

DATE (DD/MM/YY)	DEPARTURE		ARRIVAL		AIRCRAFT		NAME(S) PIC	SINGLE PILOT TIME		MULTI PILOT TIME		TOTAL TIME OF FLIGHT		NO. LDG.	
	PLACE	TIME (hh:mm)	PLACE	TIME (hh:mm)	MAKE, MODEL, VARIANT	REGISTRATION		SE	ME					DAY	NIGHT
							TOTAL FROM THIS PAGE								
							TOTAL FROM PREVIOUS PAGE								
							TOTAL TO DATE								

CONDITIONS OF FLIGHT				PILOT FUNCTION TIME				FSTD SESSION			REMARKS AND ENDORSEMENTS
NIGHT	IFR		FLIGHT RULES	PIC	CO-PILOT	DUAL	FI	DATE (DD/MM/YY)	TYPE	TOTAL TIME OF SESSION	
	HOOD	ACTUAL									
											I certify that the statements made by me on this form are true.
											PILOT'S SIGNATURE

DATE (DD/MM/YY)	DEPARTURE		ARRIVAL		AIRCRAFT		NAME(S) PIC	SINGLE PILOT TIME		MULTI PILOT TIME		TOTAL TIME OF FLIGHT		NO. LDG.	
	PLACE	TIME (hh:mm)	PLACE	TIME (hh:mm)	MAKE, MODEL, VARIANT	REGISTRATION		SE	ME					DAY	NIGHT
							TOTAL FROM THIS PAGE								
							TOTAL FROM PREVIOUS PAGE								
							TOTAL TO DATE								

CONDITIONS OF FLIGHT				PILOT FUNCTION TIME				FSTD SESSION			REMARKS AND ENDORSEMENTS
NIGHT	IFR		FLIGHT RULES	PIC	CO-PILOT	DUAL	FI	DATE (DD/MM/YY)	TYPE	TOTAL TIME OF SESSION	
	HOOD	ACTUAL									

I certify that the statements made by me on this form are true.

PILOT'S SIGNATURE

DATE (DD/MM/YY)	DEPARTURE		ARRIVAL		AIRCRAFT		NAME(S) PIC	SINGLE PILOT TIME		MULTI PILOT TIME		TOTAL TIME OF FLIGHT		NO. LDG.	
	PLACE	TIME (hh:mm)	PLACE	TIME (hh:mm)	MAKE, MODEL, VARIANT	REGISTRATION		SE	ME					DAY	NIGHT
							TOTAL FROM THIS PAGE								
							TOTAL FROM PREVIOUS PAGE								
							TOTAL TO DATE								

CONDITIONS OF FLIGHT							PILOT FUNCTION TIME								FSTD SESSION				REMARKS AND ENDORSEMENTS
NIGHT		IFR				FLIGHT RULES	PIC		CO-PILOT		DUAL		FI		DATE (DD/MM/YY)	TYPE	TOTAL TIME OF SESSION		
		HOOD		ACTUAL															
																			I certify that the statements made by me on this form are true.
																			PILOT'S SIGNATURE

DATE (DD/MM/YY)	DEPARTURE		ARRIVAL		AIRCRAFT		NAME(S) PIC	SINGLE PILOT TIME		MULTI PILOT TIME	TOTAL TIME OF FLIGHT	NO. LDG.	
	PLACE	TIME (hh:mm)	PLACE	TIME (hh:mm)	MAKE, MODEL, VARIANT	REGISTRATION		SE	ME			DAY	NIGHT
							TOTAL FROM THIS PAGE						
							TOTAL FROM PREVIOUS PAGE						
							TOTAL TO DATE						

CONDITIONS OF FLIGHT				PILOT FUNCTION TIME				FSTD SESSION			REMARKS AND ENDORSEMENTS
NIGHT	IFR		FLIGHT RULES	PIC	CO-PILOT	DUAL	FI	DATE (DD/MM/YY)	TYPE	TOTAL TIME OF SESSION	
	HOOD	ACTUAL									

I certify that the statements made by me on this form are true.

PILOT'S SIGNATURE

DATE (DD/MM/YY)	DEPARTURE		ARRIVAL		AIRCRAFT		NAME(S) PIC	SINGLE PILOT TIME		MULTI PILOT TIME		TOTAL TIME OF FLIGHT		NO. LDG.	
	PLACE	TIME (hh:mm)	PLACE	TIME (hh:mm)	MAKE, MODEL, VARIANT	REGISTRATION		SE	ME					DAY	NIGHT
							TOTAL FROM THIS PAGE								
							TOTAL FROM PREVIOUS PAGE								
							TOTAL TO DATE								

CONDITIONS OF FLIGHT							PILOT FUNCTION TIME								FSTD SESSION				REMARKS AND ENDORSEMENTS
NIGHT		IFR				FLIGHT RULES	PIC		CO-PILOT		DUAL		FI		DATE (DD/MM/YY)	TYPE	TOTAL TIME OF SESSION		
		HOOD		ACTUAL															
																			I certify that the statements made by me on this form are true.
																			PILOT'S SIGNATURE

DATE (DD/MM/YY)	DEPARTURE		ARRIVAL		AIRCRAFT		NAME(S) PIC	SINGLE PILOT TIME		MULTI PILOT TIME		TOTAL TIME OF FLIGHT		NO. LDG.	
	PLACE	TIME (hh:mm)	PLACE	TIME (hh:mm)	MAKE, MODEL, VARIANT	REGISTRATION		SE	ME					DAY	NIGHT
							TOTAL FROM THIS PAGE								
							TOTAL FROM PREVIOUS PAGE								
							TOTAL TO DATE								

CONDITIONS OF FLIGHT				PILOT FUNCTION TIME				FSTD SESSION			REMARKS AND ENDORSEMENTS
NIGHT	IFR		FLIGHT RULES	PIC	CO-PILOT	DUAL	FI	DATE (DD/MM/YY)	TYPE	TOTAL TIME OF SESSION	
	HOOD	ACTUAL									
											I certify that the statements made by me on this form are true.
											PILOT'S SIGNATURE

DATE (DD/MM/YY)	DEPARTURE		ARRIVAL		AIRCRAFT		NAME(S) PIC	SINGLE PILOT TIME		MULTI PILOT TIME		TOTAL TIME OF FLIGHT		NO. LDG.	
	PLACE	TIME (hh:mm)	PLACE	TIME (hh:mm)	MAKE, MODEL, VARIANT	REGISTRATION		SE	ME					DAY	NIGHT
							TOTAL FROM THIS PAGE								
							TOTAL FROM PREVIOUS PAGE								
							TOTAL TO DATE								

CONDITIONS OF FLIGHT				PILOT FUNCTION TIME				FSTD SESSION			REMARKS AND ENDORSEMENTS
NIGHT	IFR		FLIGHT RULES	PIC	CO-PILOT	DUAL	FI	DATE (DD/MM/YY)	TYPE	TOTAL TIME OF SESSION	
	HOOD	ACTUAL									
											I certify that the statements made by me on this form are true.
											PILOT'S SIGNATURE

DATE (DD/MM/YY)	DEPARTURE		ARRIVAL		AIRCRAFT		NAME(S) PIC	SINGLE PILOT TIME		MULTI PILOT TIME		TOTAL TIME OF FLIGHT		NO. LDG.	
	PLACE	TIME (hh:mm)	PLACE	TIME (hh:mm)	MAKE, MODEL, VARIANT	REGISTRATION		SE	ME					DAY	NIGHT
							TOTAL FROM THIS PAGE								
							TOTAL FROM PREVIOUS PAGE								
							TOTAL TO DATE								

CONDITIONS OF FLIGHT							PILOT FUNCTION TIME								FSTD SESSION				REMARKS AND ENDORSEMENTS
NIGHT		IFR				FLIGHT RULES	PIC		CO-PILOT		DUAL		FI		DATE (DD/MM/YY)	TYPE	TOTAL TIME OF SESSION		
		HOOD		ACTUAL															
																			I certify that the statements made by me on this form are true.
																			PILOT'S SIGNATURE

DATE (DD/MM/YY)	DEPARTURE		ARRIVAL		AIRCRAFT		NAME(S) PIC	SINGLE PILOT TIME		MULTI PILOT TIME		TOTAL TIME OF FLIGHT		NO. LDG.	
	PLACE	TIME (hh:mm)	PLACE	TIME (hh:mm)	MAKE, MODEL, VARIANT	REGISTRATION		SE	ME					DAY	NIGHT
							TOTAL FROM THIS PAGE								
							TOTAL FROM PREVIOUS PAGE								
							TOTAL TO DATE								

CONDITIONS OF FLIGHT				PILOT FUNCTION TIME				FSTD SESSION			REMARKS AND ENDORSEMENTS
NIGHT	IFR		FLIGHT RULES	PIC	CO-PILOT	DUAL	FI	DATE (DD/MM/YY)	TYPE	TOTAL TIME OF SESSION	
	HOOD	ACTUAL									

I certify that the statements made by me on this form are true.

PILOT'S SIGNATURE

DATE (DD/MM/YY)	DEPARTURE		ARRIVAL		AIRCRAFT		NAME(S) PIC	SINGLE PILOT TIME		MULTI PILOT TIME		TOTAL TIME OF FLIGHT		NO. LDG.	
	PLACE	TIME (hh:mm)	PLACE	TIME (hh:mm)	MAKE, MODEL, VARIANT	REGISTRATION		SE	ME					DAY	NIGHT
							TOTAL FROM THIS PAGE								
							TOTAL FROM PREVIOUS PAGE								
							TOTAL TO DATE								

CONDITIONS OF FLIGHT							PILOT FUNCTION TIME								FSTD SESSION				REMARKS AND ENDORSEMENTS
NIGHT		IFR				FLIGHT RULES	PIC		CO-PILOT		DUAL		FI		DATE (DD/MM/YY)	TYPE	TOTAL TIME OF SESSION		
		HOOD		ACTUAL															
																			I certify that the statements made by me on this form are true.
																			PILOT'S SIGNATURE

DATE (DD/MM/YY)	**DEPARTURE**		**ARRIVAL**		**AIRCRAFT**		**NAME(S) PIC**	**SINGLE PILOT TIME**		**MULTI PILOT TIME**		**TOTAL TIME OF FLIGHT**		**NO. LDG.**	
	PLACE	TIME (hh:mm)	PLACE	TIME (hh:mm)	MAKE, MODEL, VARIANT	REGISTRATION		SE	ME					DAY	NIGHT
							TOTAL FROM THIS PAGE								
							TOTAL FROM PREVIOUS PAGE								
							TOTAL TO DATE								

CONDITIONS OF FLIGHT				PILOT FUNCTION TIME				FSTD SESSION			REMARKS AND ENDORSEMENTS
NIGHT	IFR		FLIGHT RULES	PIC	CO-PILOT	DUAL	FI	DATE (DD/MM/YY)	TYPE	TOTAL TIME OF SESSION	
	HOOD	ACTUAL									
											I certify that the statements made by me on this form are true.
											PILOT'S SIGNATURE

DATE (DD/MM/YY)	DEPARTURE		ARRIVAL		AIRCRAFT		NAME(S) PIC	SINGLE PILOT TIME		MULTI PILOT TIME		TOTAL TIME OF FLIGHT		NO. LDG.	
	PLACE	TIME (hh:mm)	PLACE	TIME (hh:mm)	MAKE, MODEL, VARIANT	REGISTRATION		SE	ME					DAY	NIGHT
							TOTAL FROM THIS PAGE								
							TOTAL FROM PREVIOUS PAGE								
							TOTAL TO DATE								

CONDITIONS OF FLIGHT							PILOT FUNCTION TIME								FSTD SESSION				REMARKS AND ENDORSEMENTS
NIGHT		IFR				FLIGHT RULES	PIC		CO-PILOT		DUAL		FI		DATE (DD/MM/YY)	TYPE	TOTAL TIME OF SESSION		
		HOOD		ACTUAL															
																			I certify that the statements made by me on this form are true.
																			PILOT'S SIGNATURE

DATE (DD/MM/YY)	DEPARTURE		ARRIVAL		AIRCRAFT		NAME(S) PIC	SINGLE PILOT TIME		MULTI PILOT TIME	TOTAL TIME OF FLIGHT	NO. LDG.	
	PLACE	TIME (hh:mm)	PLACE	TIME (hh:mm)	MAKE, MODEL, VARIANT	REGISTRATION		SE	ME			DAY	NIGHT
							TOTAL FROM THIS PAGE						
							TOTAL FROM PREVIOUS PAGE						
							TOTAL TO DATE						

CONDITIONS OF FLIGHT				PILOT FUNCTION TIME				FSTD SESSION			REMARKS AND ENDORSEMENTS
NIGHT	IFR		FLIGHT RULES	PIC	CO-PILOT	DUAL	FI	DATE (DD/MM/YY)	TYPE	TOTAL TIME OF SESSION	
	HOOD	ACTUAL									
											I certify that the statements made by me on this form are true.
											PILOT'S SIGNATURE

DATE (DD/MM/YY)	DEPARTURE		ARRIVAL		AIRCRAFT		NAME(S) PIC	SINGLE PILOT TIME		MULTI PILOT TIME		TOTAL TIME OF FLIGHT		NO. LDG.	
	PLACE	TIME (hh:mm)	PLACE	TIME (hh:mm)	MAKE, MODEL, VARIANT	REGISTRATION		SE	ME					DAY	NIGHT
							TOTAL FROM THIS PAGE								
							TOTAL FROM PREVIOUS PAGE								
							TOTAL TO DATE								

CONDITIONS OF FLIGHT				PILOT FUNCTION TIME				FSTD SESSION			REMARKS AND ENDORSEMENTS
NIGHT	IFR		FLIGHT RULES	PIC	CO-PILOT	DUAL	FI	DATE (DD/MM/YY)	TYPE	TOTAL TIME OF SESSION	
	HOOD	ACTUAL									
											I certify that the statements made by me on this form are true.
											PILOT'S SIGNATURE

DATE (DD/MM/YY)	DEPARTURE		ARRIVAL		AIRCRAFT		NAME(S) PIC	SINGLE PILOT TIME		MULTI PILOT TIME		TOTAL TIME OF FLIGHT		NO. LDG.	
	PLACE	TIME (hh:mm)	PLACE	TIME (hh:mm)	MAKE, MODEL, VARIANT	REGISTRATION		SE	ME					DAY	NIGHT
							TOTAL FROM THIS PAGE								
							TOTAL FROM PREVIOUS PAGE								
							TOTAL TO DATE								

CONDITIONS OF FLIGHT				PILOT FUNCTION TIME				FSTD SESSION			REMARKS AND ENDORSEMENTS
NIGHT	IFR		FLIGHT RULES	PIC	CO-PILOT	DUAL	FI	DATE (DD/MM/YY)	TYPE	TOTAL TIME OF SESSION	
	HOOD	ACTUAL									
											I certify that the statements made by me on this form are true.
											PILOT'S SIGNATURE

DATE (DD/MM/YY)	DEPARTURE		ARRIVAL		AIRCRAFT		NAME(S) PIC	SINGLE PILOT TIME		MULTI PILOT TIME		TOTAL TIME OF FLIGHT		NO. LDG.	
	PLACE	TIME (hh:mm)	PLACE	TIME (hh:mm)	MAKE, MODEL, VARIANT	REGISTRATION		SE	ME					DAY	NIGHT
							TOTAL FROM THIS PAGE								
							TOTAL FROM PREVIOUS PAGE								
							TOTAL TO DATE								

CONDITIONS OF FLIGHT							PILOT FUNCTION TIME								FSTD SESSION				REMARKS AND ENDORSEMENTS
NIGHT		IFR				FLIGHT RULES	PIC		CO-PILOT		DUAL		FI		DATE (DD/MM/YY)	TYPE	TOTAL TIME OF SESSION		
		HOOD		ACTUAL															
																			I certify that the statements made by me on this form are true.
																			PILOT'S SIGNATURE

DATE (DD/MM/YY)	DEPARTURE		ARRIVAL		AIRCRAFT		NAME(S) PIC	SINGLE PILOT TIME		MULTI PILOT TIME		TOTAL TIME OF FLIGHT		NO. LDG.	
	PLACE	TIME (hh:mm)	PLACE	TIME (hh:mm)	MAKE, MODEL, VARIANT	REGISTRATION		SE	ME					DAY	NIGHT
							TOTAL FROM THIS PAGE								
							TOTAL FROM PREVIOUS PAGE								
							TOTAL TO DATE								

CONDITIONS OF FLIGHT				PILOT FUNCTION TIME				FSTD SESSION			REMARKS AND ENDORSEMENTS
NIGHT	IFR		FLIGHT RULES	PIC	CO-PILOT	DUAL	FI	DATE (DD/MM/YY)	TYPE	TOTAL TIME OF SESSION	
	HOOD	ACTUAL									
											I certify that the statements made by me on this form are true.
											PILOT'S SIGNATURE

DATE (DD/MM/YY)	DEPARTURE		ARRIVAL		AIRCRAFT		NAME(S) PIC	SINGLE PILOT TIME		MULTI PILOT TIME		TOTAL TIME OF FLIGHT		NO. LDG.	
	PLACE	TIME (hh:mm)	PLACE	TIME (hh:mm)	MAKE, MODEL, VARIANT	REGISTRATION		SE	ME					DAY	NIGHT
							TOTAL FROM THIS PAGE								
							TOTAL FROM PREVIOUS PAGE								
							TOTAL TO DATE								

CONDITIONS OF FLIGHT				PILOT FUNCTION TIME				FSTD SESSION			REMARKS AND ENDORSEMENTS
NIGHT	IFR		FLIGHT RULES	PIC	CO-PILOT	DUAL	FI	DATE (DD/MM/YY)	TYPE	TOTAL TIME OF SESSION	
	HOOD	ACTUAL									
											I certify that the statements made by me on this form are true.
											PILOT'S SIGNATURE

DATE (DD/MM/YY)	DEPARTURE		ARRIVAL		AIRCRAFT		NAME(S) PIC	SINGLE PILOT TIME		MULTI PILOT TIME		TOTAL TIME OF FLIGHT		NO. LDG.	
	PLACE	TIME (hh:mm)	PLACE	TIME (hh:mm)	MAKE, MODEL, VARIANT	REGISTRATION		SE	ME					DAY	NIGHT
							TOTAL FROM THIS PAGE								
							TOTAL FROM PREVIOUS PAGE								
							TOTAL TO DATE								

CONDITIONS OF FLIGHT							PILOT FUNCTION TIME								FSTD SESSION				REMARKS AND ENDORSEMENTS
NIGHT		IFR				FLIGHT RULES	PIC		CO-PILOT		DUAL		FI		DATE (DD/MM/YY)	TYPE	TOTAL TIME OF SESSION		
		HOOD		ACTUAL															
																			I certify that the statements made by me on this form are true.
																			PILOT'S SIGNATURE

DATE (DD/MM/YY)	DEPARTURE		ARRIVAL		AIRCRAFT		NAME(S) PIC	SINGLE PILOT TIME		MULTI PILOT TIME		TOTAL TIME OF FLIGHT		NO. LDG.	
	PLACE	TIME (hh:mm)	PLACE	TIME (hh:mm)	MAKE, MODEL, VARIANT	REGISTRATION		SE	ME					DAY	NIGHT
							TOTAL FROM THIS PAGE								
							TOTAL FROM PREVIOUS PAGE								
							TOTAL TO DATE								

CONDITIONS OF FLIGHT				PILOT FUNCTION TIME				FSTD SESSION			REMARKS AND ENDORSEMENTS
NIGHT	IFR		FLIGHT RULES	PIC	CO-PILOT	DUAL	FI	DATE (DD/MM/YY)	TYPE	TOTAL TIME OF SESSION	
	HOOD	ACTUAL									

I certify that the statements made by me on this form are true.

PILOT'S SIGNATURE

DATE (DD/MM/YY)	DEPARTURE		ARRIVAL		AIRCRAFT		NAME(S) PIC	SINGLE PILOT TIME		MULTI PILOT TIME		TOTAL TIME OF FLIGHT		NO. LDG.	
	PLACE	TIME (hh:mm)	PLACE	TIME (hh:mm)	MAKE, MODEL, VARIANT	REGISTRATION		SE	ME					DAY	NIGHT
							TOTAL FROM THIS PAGE								
							TOTAL FROM PREVIOUS PAGE								
							TOTAL TO DATE								

CONDITIONS OF FLIGHT				PILOT FUNCTION TIME				FSTD SESSION			REMARKS AND ENDORSEMENTS
NIGHT	IFR		FLIGHT RULES	PIC	CO-PILOT	DUAL	FI	DATE (DD/MM/YY)	TYPE	TOTAL TIME OF SESSION	
	HOOD	ACTUAL									
											I certify that the statements made by me on this form are true.
											PILOT'S SIGNATURE

DATE (DD/MM/YY)	DEPARTURE		ARRIVAL		AIRCRAFT		NAME(S) PIC	SINGLE PILOT TIME		MULTI PILOT TIME		TOTAL TIME OF FLIGHT		NO. LDG.	
	PLACE	TIME (hh:mm)	PLACE	TIME (hh:mm)	MAKE, MODEL, VARIANT	REGISTRATION		SE	ME					DAY	NIGHT
							TOTAL FROM THIS PAGE								
							TOTAL FROM PREVIOUS PAGE								
							TOTAL TO DATE								

CONDITIONS OF FLIGHT				PILOT FUNCTION TIME				FSTD SESSION			REMARKS AND ENDORSEMENTS
NIGHT	IFR HOOD	IFR ACTUAL	FLIGHT RULES	PIC	CO-PILOT	DUAL	FI	DATE (DD/MM/YY)	TYPE	TOTAL TIME OF SESSION	
											I certify that the statements made by me on this form are true.
											PILOT'S SIGNATURE

DATE (DD/MM/YY)	DEPARTURE		ARRIVAL		AIRCRAFT		NAME(S) PIC	SINGLE PILOT TIME		MULTI PILOT TIME		TOTAL TIME OF FLIGHT		NO. LDG.	
	PLACE	TIME (hh:mm)	PLACE	TIME (hh:mm)	MAKE, MODEL, VARIANT	REGISTRATION		SE	ME					DAY	NIGHT
							TOTAL FROM THIS PAGE								
							TOTAL FROM PREVIOUS PAGE								
							TOTAL TO DATE								

CONDITIONS OF FLIGHT							PILOT FUNCTION TIME								FSTD SESSION				REMARKS AND ENDORSEMENTS
NIGHT		IFR				FLIGHT RULES	PIC		CO-PILOT		DUAL		FI		DATE (DD/MM/YY)	TYPE	TOTAL TIME OF SESSION		
		HOOD		ACTUAL															

I certify that the statements made by me on this form are true.

PILOT'S SIGNATURE

DATE (DD/MM/YY)	DEPARTURE		ARRIVAL		AIRCRAFT		NAME(S) PIC	SINGLE PILOT TIME		MULTI PILOT TIME		TOTAL TIME OF FLIGHT		NO. LDG.	
	PLACE	TIME (hh:mm)	PLACE	TIME (hh:mm)	MAKE, MODEL, VARIANT	REGISTRATION		SE	ME					DAY	NIGHT
							TOTAL FROM THIS PAGE								
							TOTAL FROM PREVIOUS PAGE								
							TOTAL TO DATE								

CONDITIONS OF FLIGHT				PILOT FUNCTION TIME				FSTD SESSION			REMARKS AND ENDORSEMENTS
NIGHT	IFR		FLIGHT RULES	PIC	CO-PILOT	DUAL	FI	DATE (DD/MM/YY)	TYPE	TOTAL TIME OF SESSION	
	HOOD	ACTUAL									

I certify that the statements made by me on this form are true.

PILOT'S SIGNATURE

DATE (DD/MM/YY)	DEPARTURE		ARRIVAL		AIRCRAFT		NAME(S) PIC	SINGLE PILOT TIME		MULTI PILOT TIME		TOTAL TIME OF FLIGHT		NO. LDG.	
	PLACE	TIME (hh:mm)	PLACE	TIME (hh:mm)	MAKE, MODEL, VARIANT	REGISTRATION		SE	ME					DAY	NIGHT
							TOTAL FROM THIS PAGE								
							TOTAL FROM PREVIOUS PAGE								
							TOTAL TO DATE								

CONDITIONS OF FLIGHT							**PILOT FUNCTION TIME**								**FSTD SESSION**				**REMARKS AND ENDORSEMENTS**
NIGHT		IFR				FLIGHT RULES	PIC		CO-PILOT		DUAL		FI		DATE (DD/MM/YY)	TYPE	TOTAL TIME OF SESSION		
		HOOD		ACTUAL															
																			I certify that the statements made by me on this form are true.
																			PILOT'S SIGNATURE

DATE (DD/MM/YY)	DEPARTURE		ARRIVAL		AIRCRAFT		NAME(S) PIC	SINGLE PILOT TIME		MULTI PILOT TIME		TOTAL TIME OF FLIGHT		NO. LDG.	
	PLACE	TIME (hh:mm)	PLACE	TIME (hh:mm)	MAKE, MODEL, VARIANT	REGISTRATION		SE	ME					DAY	NIGHT
							TOTAL FROM THIS PAGE								
							TOTAL FROM PREVIOUS PAGE								
							TOTAL TO DATE								

CONDITIONS OF FLIGHT				PILOT FUNCTION TIME				FSTD SESSION			REMARKS AND ENDORSEMENTS
NIGHT	IFR		FLIGHT RULES	PIC	CO-PILOT	DUAL	FI	DATE (DD/MM/YY)	TYPE	TOTAL TIME OF SESSION	
	HOOD	ACTUAL									
											I certify that the statements made by me on this form are true.
											PILOT'S SIGNATURE

DATE (DD/MM/YY)	DEPARTURE		ARRIVAL		AIRCRAFT		NAME(S) PIC	SINGLE PILOT TIME		MULTI PILOT TIME		TOTAL TIME OF FLIGHT		NO. LDG.	
	PLACE	TIME (hh:mm)	PLACE	TIME (hh:mm)	MAKE, MODEL, VARIANT	REGISTRATION		SE	ME					DAY	NIGHT
							TOTAL FROM THIS PAGE								
							TOTAL FROM PREVIOUS PAGE								
							TOTAL TO DATE								

CONDITIONS OF FLIGHT							PILOT FUNCTION TIME								FSTD SESSION				REMARKS AND ENDORSEMENTS
NIGHT		IFR				FLIGHT RULES	PIC		CO-PILOT		DUAL		FI		DATE (DD/MM/YY)	TYPE	TOTAL TIME OF SESSION		
		HOOD		ACTUAL															
																			I certify that the statements made by me on this form are true.
																			PILOT'S SIGNATURE

DATE (DD/MM/YY)	DEPARTURE		ARRIVAL		AIRCRAFT		NAME(S) PIC	SINGLE PILOT TIME		MULTI PILOT TIME		TOTAL TIME OF FLIGHT		NO. LDG.	
	PLACE	TIME (hh:mm)	PLACE	TIME (hh:mm)	MAKE, MODEL, VARIANT	REGISTRATION		SE	ME					DAY	NIGHT
							TOTAL FROM THIS PAGE								
							TOTAL FROM PREVIOUS PAGE								
							TOTAL TO DATE								

CONDITIONS OF FLIGHT				PILOT FUNCTION TIME				FSTD SESSION			REMARKS AND ENDORSEMENTS
NIGHT	IFR		FLIGHT RULES	PIC	CO-PILOT	DUAL	FI	DATE (DD/MM/YY)	TYPE	TOTAL TIME OF SESSION	
	HOOD	ACTUAL									
											I certify that the statements made by me on this form are true.
											PILOT'S SIGNATURE

DATE (DD/MM/YY)	DEPARTURE		ARRIVAL		AIRCRAFT		NAME(S) PIC	SINGLE PILOT TIME		MULTI PILOT TIME		TOTAL TIME OF FLIGHT		NO. LDG.	
	PLACE	TIME (hh:mm)	PLACE	TIME (hh:mm)	MAKE, MODEL, VARIANT	REGISTRATION		SE	ME					DAY	NIGHT
							TOTAL FROM THIS PAGE								
							TOTAL FROM PREVIOUS PAGE								
							TOTAL TO DATE								

CONDITIONS OF FLIGHT							PILOT FUNCTION TIME								FSTD SESSION				REMARKS AND ENDORSEMENTS
NIGHT		IFR				FLIGHT RULES	PIC		CO-PILOT		DUAL		FI		DATE (DD/MM/YY)	TYPE	TOTAL TIME OF SESSION		
		HOOD		ACTUAL															
																			I certify that the statements made by me on this form are true.
																			PILOT'S SIGNATURE

Licences, Ratings and Types

DATE OF ISSUE	PERMIT/LICENCE/RATING/TYPE	NUMBER	EXAMINER/AUTHORITY	REMARKS

Proficiencies, Reviews and Medicals

DATE OF ISSUE	TYPE OF PC/REVIEW/MEDICAL	NUMBER	EXAMINER/AUTHORITY	REMARKS

GROUND INSTRUCTION LOG

DATE	LESSON PLAN	INSTRUCTOR	TIME	TOTAL

GROUND INSTRUCTION LOG

DATE	LESSON PLAN	INSTRUCTOR	TIME	TOTAL

YEAR 20 ____	CLASSIFICATION OF PILOT-IN-COMMAND TIME												
	JAN.	FEB.	MAR.	APR.	MAY	JUNE	JULY	AUG.	SEPT.	OCT.	NOV.	DEC.	TOTAL
SINGLE ENGINE													
MULTI-ENGINE													
TURBINE ENGINE													
CROSS-COUNTRY													
NIGHT													
GROUND TRAINER													
SIMULATED INSTRUMENT													
ACTUAL INSTRUMENT													
UNCREWED (UAS)													

YEAR 20 ____	CLASSIFICATION OF PILOT-IN-COMMAND TIME												
	JAN.	FEB.	MAR.	APR.	MAY	JUNE	JULY	AUG.	SEPT.	OCT.	NOV.	DEC.	TOTAL
SINGLE ENGINE													
MULTI-ENGINE													
TURBINE ENGINE													
CROSS-COUNTRY													
NIGHT													
GROUND TRAINER													
SIMULATED INSTRUMENT													
ACTUAL INSTRUMENT													
UNCREWED (UAS)													

AIRCRAFT FLOWN AND NUMBER OF HOURS IN EACH

AIRCRAFT MAKE AND MODEL	PIC	DUAL REC'D.	AIRCRAFT MAKE AND MODEL	PIC	DUAL REC'D.

Conversion of Minutes to Decimals

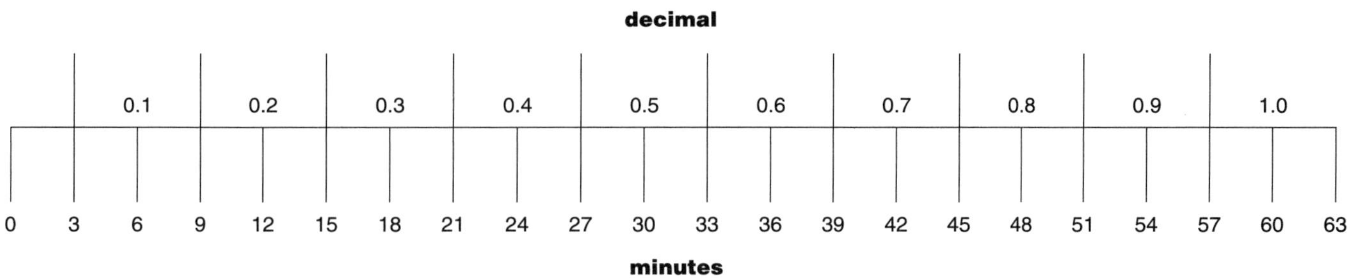

NOTES